PASSION IN THE BONES

PASSION
IN THE
BONES

A GUIDE TO BREAKING THE CHAINS OF NEGATIVITY
AND LIVING YOUR OWN ADVENTURE

ELAINE HOWARD

Radius Book Group
New York

Distributed by Radius Book Group
A Division of Diversion Publishing Corp.
443 Park Avenue South, Suite 1004
New York, NY 10016
www.RadiusBookGroup.com

Library of Congress Control Number: 2018958127

For more information, email info@radiusbookgroup.com.

First edition: January 2019
Trade Paperback ISBN: 978-1-63576-588-5
eBook ISBN: 978-1-63576-589-2

Manufactured in the United States of America

10 9 8 7 6 5 4 3 2 1

Cover design by Mark Karis, Neuwirth & Associates
Interior design by Elyse Strongin, Neuwirth & Associates

Radius Book Group and the Radius Book Group colophon are registered
trademarks of Radius Book Group, a Division of Diversion Publishing Corp.

This book is dedicated to those who feel they do not fit in.
Celebrate your individuality and use it to make
a positive difference in the world.

CONTENTS

FOREWORD

by Dean R. Lomax

In the summer of 2008, after saving enough funds to visit the United States for the first time, I met Elaine Howard at the Wyoming Dinosaur Center in Thermopolis, Wyoming. At the time, I was an eighteen-year-old from Britain pursuing my plan to become a professional palaeontologist, and Elaine was a lawyer from Florida. Despite our differences (including how I spell *palaeontology*, and she spells *paleontology*), Elaine and I made an instant connection based entirely upon our shared love of fossils. In fact, one of my fond memories was at a Chinese restaurant where we talked all evening about everything dinosaur until they kicked us out after closing time. More than a decade later, we remain close friends who try to never miss an opportunity to share our mutual love for all things prehistoric.

Over the years, Elaine and I have often discussed the power and importance of having a passion in life. By following mine, I achieved my goal to become a successful palaeontologist, and by following hers, Elaine transformed her life from one centered around her feelings of hopelessness and unfulfillment to one of excitement, adventure, and discovery.

In *Passion in the Bones*, Elaine takes a closer look at the concept of passion, why finding hers had a significant impact on her life, and how anyone can transform his or her life for the better by not just finding passion, but also by sharing and sustaining it. Elaine reveals what she has learned from her own experience and shares the inspiring stories of other positive people who live life to the fullest by pursuing their passion. Through her own unique, dinosaur-themed style, she provides exciting and fascinating insights into her journey of discovery.

If you find yourself focused on negative circumstances, this book will remind you that YOU have the power to enjoy life and make the most of it. Passion provides us with a purpose. Life is better when you do what you love, and Elaine's story shows just how your life can be changed if you're willing to follow your passion. Perhaps most important, the book offers valuable insights into how to unleash that power and live the positive and fulfilling life you deserve.

—DEAN R. LOMAX
Palaeontologist, Author, and Science Communicator
Visiting Scientist, The University of Manchester, UK
www.deanrlomax.co.uk
Twitter: @Dean_R_Lomax

PASSION IN THE BONES

INTRODUCTION

Even as a young child, I felt out of place. My father was a crop duster whose unusual occupation required us to move with the agricultural seasons and as my father could find work. We bounced around from Florida to North Carolina to Mississippi and beyond. By the time I was in middle school, I had attended at least seven different schools. I would just start to make friends by the time we had to move again.

Childhood was lonely. With all the moving around and frequently being the "new kid" in class, I desperately wished I had a sibling who would be my friend and playmate wherever we moved. That did not happen. My mother always wanted a daughter, so from the time I was born, she tried her best to mold me into the frilly little girl she wanted me to be. The older I grew, however, the more obvious it became I did not fit that mold.

In school, I struggled to keep up. Without considering the root of my problem, several schools labeled me as a slow learner. I was subsequently moved to a more advanced class where I managed to get by, although I still had difficulty with math, science, and writing. Because my grades continued to fluctuate, my teachers were not sure what to make of me. By then, I was not sure what to make of myself.

Figure 1. Our home in Mississippi

At the time, I ate to cope with my stress and ended up with a little too much weight for my height. That led to teasing, which led to more stress.

By seventh grade, I was a little overwhelmed and exhausted and had decided I was no more than average. I still did not fit in academically, socially, and certainly not athletically. Although I had lost a little weight by then, I was still shorter than average with little muscle tone, so I was always the last to be picked for any team. That did not help my self-esteem.

As difficult as those days were, I had one ray of light and spark of inspiration. In a sea of awkward middle school students, there was one girl in my class in Haines City, Florida, who had a voice like I had never heard before, and she was not afraid to use it. I would hear her singing in math class, gym class, and even on the school bus. And, when she wasn't entertaining us at school, she was singing in her father's church. Her name was Sisaundra Lewis, and she was everything I was not. She was talented and outgoing, and when she started to sing, students and teachers alike would listen in amazement to this huge voice coming from such a young girl. Outside of school and church, Sisaundra picked fruit in the Florida orange groves with her family. Despite such hard and exhausting work, she maintained a positive attitude and was a lot of fun to be around even when she wasn't singing. It was clear Sisaundra found her passion at an incredibly young age.

Sisaundra not only entertained those around her, she also lifted their spirits. Witnessing my childhood friend inspire and entertain people gave me an early glimpse of how important it is to find something you enjoy and share it with others. Discovering my own passion—in my mid-thirties—truly opened my eyes to how life-changing it can be.

Perhaps you came to this book because you feel like you're stuck in a rut and need help getting out. Perhaps you find yourself too focused on negativity and want to turn that around. Whatever the reason, I'm glad you're here.

Let me start by asking you a question: Do you find yourself focusing on whatever is going wrong in your life? Perhaps you are worried about problems at work or home. Or, perhaps you feel you are losing hope that a void in your life (a relationship, child, career opportunity, etc.) will ever be filled, and you have allowed your doubt and fear to take over. It is human nature to focus on our negative circumstances. But it is important to understand that whatever we focus on—negative or positive—is what tends to manifest in our lives.

When our minds are filled with worry, doubt, and fear, our negative thoughts produce negative energy, which, in turn, draws more negativity into our lives and makes it very difficult for our circumstances to improve. When our minds are focused on something positive and exciting, however, our enthusiasm creates a positive energy, which not only improves the quality of our lives but also draws positive people and opportunities to us. Indeed, a positive mental focus not only helps break the cycle of negativity, it initiates a cycle of positivity in our lives.

So, if your mind is filled with worry, doubt, and fear, how on earth do you focus on something positive and exciting? Good question! A powerful way to do that—to ensure you manifest the best things possible for your life—is by finding and following your PASSION.

I know this is to be true because, for more than a decade, I focused on what I felt was missing in my life and, as a result, I felt an overwhelming sense of hopelessness. There were even times when I contemplated and even planned to "end it all." I did not realize that my negative focus was drawing more negativity into my life and making it virtually impossible for my dreams to unfold.

That all changed in 2005, when I inadvertently discovered my passion for paleontology. My life soon transformed from one of despair and hopelessness to one of excitement and adventure. On the surface, it appeared as though dinosaurs brought me back to life. In reality, it was not dinosaurs that changed my life, but my change in mental focus that broke the cycle of negativity and radically transformed my life for the better. I now realize that every person I know who is happy and lives life to the fullest is, on some level, pursuing his or her passion.

Some suggest that your passion is the one true calling that you should strive to make your career. Others say that your passion is not "one thing" you pursue but something you find within yourself. In fact, the word *passion* has various meanings, including a strong emotion (be it love or hatred) or an intense desire for another person, just to name a few.

None of that really explains what happened to me. So, I started to dig deep into my own story to get some answers, not just for myself but for the many others who have expressed to me how much they wish they could find something that would change their lives for the better the way paleontology changed mine.

After years of analyzing my own journey and the lives of those who inspire me the most, I have put together this simple guide to help readers like you discover your own life-changing passion.

If you are struggling with a mental health issue, there is no substitute for professional help. I encourage you to seek evaluation and treatment from a mental health professional. If, however, your thoughts are simply focused on negativity, this book will provide you with a step-by-step guide to finding and sustaining a passion that will get the positives flowing— and keep them flowing—in your life.

If you've picked up this book, it shows you already have a vested interest in adding more positivity to your life—kudos to you for taking the initiative! Let's take this journey together. Just as paleontologists discover and unearth dinosaur bones, let's go find and uncover your passion and get you started on your own life-changing adventure.

Throughout this book, we will review case studies about the passion journeys of specific people and how they are not only reaping the benefits of their passion pursuits, but also sharing their positivity with the world.

1

BEFORE THE DINOSAURS

(MY ROAD TO FINDING PASSION)

ife can be a series of ups and downs. There are good periods, not-so-good periods, and bad I-just-have-to-survive-this periods. I've seen my fair share of each. In my early years, I had a few interests, but I certainly wasn't thinking of the link between living a passionate life and living a happy one. I was merely trying to survive.

Growing up an only child who moved around a lot and didn't seem to quite fit in, my childhood was a lonely one, but it was not without some bright spots. In an effort to lift my spirits, my parents would take me fun places—from the beach to the zoo to the county fair. My dad also let me tag along with him on his fishing trips. And every year, my parents would save up the money to take me to Walt Disney World for my birthday. That yearly trip became my brief escape from reality. I also had my special friendship with Sisaundra.

For better or worse, at the end of my eighth-grade year, my father accepted a job as the chief pilot for a farm in Zellwood, Florida, which was quite a distance from our then-home in Dundee, Florida. That meant we would have to move yet again. Recognizing my pain, my parents promised me that this job would be more stable, so I should be able to attend all four years of high school in one place. That sounded good, but it would be a new school. I would have to say goodbye to Sisaundra and a few other friends I had made in Haines City. My parents bought a double-wide mobile home down a long, dirt road in Astatula, Florida, and enrolled me in the closest high school, which was in Tavares, just a few miles away.

Figure 2. Our home in Astatula, Florida

The thought of starting high school in a totally strange place was scary. But I had decided to be an average C student and try to fly under the radar, so I did not feel much pressure to succeed. I just wanted to make average grades, hopefully make a few friends, and just "get by." Besides, it was 1983, and I had more important things on my mind, like learning to moonwalk.

The first few months in a new school where I did not know anyone were challenging. Before long, my teachers began to foil my plan for mediocrity. For some odd and inexplicable reason, my teachers—including my algebra, English, and science teachers—believed I was more than average. I don't know if they saw something in me or they were just trying to set me on the right path, but they made sure to give me positive feedback whenever possible. That was new for me, and I found myself not wanting to disappoint them.

Fortunately, not only were my high school teachers supportive, they also had a knack for making subjects, which had previously seemed like a mystery to me, easy to understand. My math teacher, Mr. Belton, who was also the town bail bondsman, presented algebra in such a way that it actually made sense, and my English teacher, Mrs. Crumpton, helped me develop strong writing skills. While I did not realize it at the time, my science teacher, Mr. Wettstein, not only helped me understand science, he planted the seed for my interest in paleontology, which would bloom many years later.

MY EARLY INTERESTS

While I had not yet discovered my own true passion, I did have several deeply rooted interests that had an impact on my life.

As a teen, beyond schoolwork, I was also focused on karate and music. Karate kept me mentally focused and, as for music, I was just a teenager who was really into the '80s music scene. I bought every record album I could afford and attended every concert within reasonable driving distance. I did not get my driver's license until my senior year, so I had to rely on my parents to transport me (and a few of my friends) to concerts. My parents enjoyed the music as well, so they actually bought tickets and went to the concerts, too. (Well, perhaps they also wanted to keep a watchful eye over me.) My parents were young—only in their thirties at the time—so it did not seem that odd, at least to me, to have them at the concerts with me. Plus, they are fun people, and I've always enjoyed hanging around them. My friends did not seem to mind either. I had (and still have) an eclectic taste in music, so we went to see every artist possible: Michael Jackson, Prince, Madonna, Tina Turner, Billy Joel, Stevie Nicks, Bon Jovi, Genesis, Rod Stewart, and Rick Springfield, to name a very few.

Music was so exciting to me that I decided by the mid-'80s I wanted to become a rock guitarist. While my mother may not have been thrilled with the idea, she signed me up for guitar lessons at a local music store. I'm sure the guitar teacher was trying to give me a good foundation, but she taught me to play really boring songs, and I lost interest very quickly. At that rate, it was going to take me years to learn to play the songs I enjoyed. I needed a new teacher, someone who could teach me how to play rock music. After an exhaustive search, my mom and I found a music school in Longwood, Florida, that taught rock guitar. Although the school was an hour's drive from our home in Astatula, my mom knew we had found something really special, so she agreed to drive me there on a weekly basis.

When I arrived for my first lesson, I was surprised that my new guitar teacher—a twenty-one-year-old named Chris Juergensen—looked like a rock star and could play my favorite songs effortlessly. He made it look so easy. He showed me some basics and explained how learning the basics was essential for learning rock guitar. Before long, I could play songs from my favorite rock bands. It was amazing how someone so young had such a gift for teaching music. I took guitar lessons from Chris for a couple years, and he proved to be not only an incredible music teacher, but also a wonderful source of inspiration and motivation for me. He also taught me another big life lesson: With my drive and dedication, I could be anything I wanted to be in life. My parents had told me that before, but to hear it from someone like Chris made it sink in and confirmed what my parents had been telling me all along.

But with the highs of life come some great lows, too. One particular day, I arrived for my guitar lesson and received some unexpected news from Chris. He had decided it was time for him to move to Los Angeles to seriously pursue his opportunities out there. That news hit me like a ton of bricks. I was so sad to hear he was leaving. By that point, I felt Chris was not only my guitar teacher, but also a friend and great source of encouragement in my life. As sad as the news was, however, I completely understood Chris's decision to follow his dreams and admired him for taking such a big leap. Chris was definitely someone who had found his passion in life and was pursuing it wholeheartedly.

Chris Juergensen

When Chris Juergensen taught me guitar lessons at a small music school in Central Florida, he was barely twenty-one years old. Chris not only had a gift for playing and teaching guitar, he had a gift for inspiring others to realize their own potential. I now understand that Chris's passion for his craft and his focus on being the best guitar player and teacher he could be created a cycle of positivity in his life that made him a true inspiration, even at such a young age. Chris subsequently moved to Los Angeles, where he established himself as a successful studio musician, session guitarist, and clinician. His success there opened the door for him to become the vice principal of the Tokyo School of Music in Tokyo, Japan, where he lived for twenty-five years. Additionally, Chris has released several critically acclaimed albums, and his music has been used in a number of movies and commercials. And if that wasn't enough, Chris has written several popular books, including *The Infinite Guitar*, as well as *The Empowered Musician* and the *Infinite Guitar Companion*. He currently divides his time between the Collective School of Music in Manhattan and the Tokyo School of Music, and he continues to educate and inspire musicians around the world.

Figure 3. Chris Juergensen in concert

Although I still loved music, after Chris moved away, I stopped taking music lessons and gave up on my dream of becoming a rock star. I set a more realistic career goal for myself and decided to become an attorney. One of the people who inspired me to make that decision was my classmate and good friend, Basil Bain, a young fellow from the Bahamas. While my career goals changed multiple times in high school, Basil made the decision to become an attorney at fourteen years old and was determined to make it happen. No, it would not be an easy road for Basil, who came from a family of twelve children. But young Basil had all he needed to succeed: mental focus, determination, and the willingness to work hard, which I later learned are the keys to success.

In our senior year of high school, Basil and I were voted by our fellow classmates as "Most Likely to Succeed." I was confident that Basil would live up to that title; I only hoped I could do the same. A few people told me that, if I opted to go to community college instead of a university, I was unlikely to follow through with my plan to go to law school. I learned right then that, while it is good to hear the advice of others, I would have to make my own path in life and do it the way that was best for me. Besides, I have a cousin who went to a community college on his road to becoming an attorney, so I knew it was possible.

After graduating second in my class, I followed in my cousin's footsteps and attended my local community college before transferring to a university. That proved to be the right decision for me, because it gave me the confidence to know I could handle college. It was also nice to have a few friends there, including Basil and other classmates.

Basil Bain

Had I not attended high school with Basil Bain, I am not sure if I would have chosen to become an attorney. I was so impressed with Basil's determination to become a lawyer that it sounded like a good career choice for me as well. As I transferred to Florida State University, Basil transferred to the University of Florida where he went on to earn his bachelor's degree and then a degree in law and accounting. Today, he is a board-certified business litigation attorney with his own successful law practice in Naples, Florida. When I told Basil about finding my passion for paleontology, he told me how happy he was that I had found such an interesting pursuit. He then said that, while it may not be as intriguing as dinosaurs, his passion was law and helping people understand their legal rights. He's a lawyer with a passion for law. Basil's passion, which he has had since he was fourteen years old, led him to become not only a successful attorney but one of the most positive people I know.

Figure 4. Board-certified business litigation attorney Basil Bain

MY DEADLY PURSUIT

After earning my associate's degree, I transferred to Florida State University. At FSU, I excelled academically but never quite fit in with the university lifestyle or the other students. I was still determined to succeed, but my self-esteem began to decline. I was lonely, but too socially awkward to join in with the other students. I thought: "Well, I'm not here to socialize, anyway. I'm here to get my degree." And that is what I did. I did not let anything stop me—even an eating disorder, which I developed during my second year at FSU.

It began as a desire to lose a few pounds to feel good about myself. I had dieted on and off during my teenage years, but there was something about that particular time at university when I noticed I was losing weight, and I felt a sense of empowerment after shedding a few pounds. So, I just kept losing and losing. I started out in April 1990 weighing 132 pounds (which I now realize was a healthy and normal weight for my frame and height), but by Christmas of that year, I was down to 80 pounds. My family was afraid I would die.

I can't really explain what went on in my mind at that time. At first, it felt good to know I was shedding a few pounds and looking "lost" in my clothes. However, there came a point when I realized I was no longer healthy as my bones protruded from my skin and my teeth became very brittle. I remember one of my teeth broke off as I was simply eating a cracker. Besides the toll dieting took on my physical health, it also wreaked havoc on my nervous system. I was continually nervous and would often lash out at others or cry hysterically for no reason.

Although I was aware my extreme dieting was unhealthy, losing weight had taken over my mindset, and I could not seem to break free of it. When I went out in public, I noticed people staring, but the gawks did not bother me. They just confirmed to me that I had lost a lot of weight. My weight loss had become more important to me than my appearance.

Many of my FSU classmates looked at me with concern but refrained from commenting about my weight. However, one classmate was bold enough to approach me in the restroom and asked if I was ill. I told her I had just lost weight from dieting. She appeared confused and unsure of what to say. It did not bother me that my classmate thought I was ill; in fact, I was proud she had noticed how much weight I had lost. It was around that time that my parents sat me down and told me that they had decided to seek professional help for me, which I knew might include entering an eating disorder clinic.

I was surprised and upset to hear them say that, but I knew they loved me and could not watch me continue on a path of self-destruction. Not only had I allowed myself to become too thin, I had developed eating habits that did not provide me with the proper nutrition to survive on a long-term basis. Although I knew my parents had my best interest at heart, I protested their plan to seek professional help, as doing so would interrupt my set timeframe for obtaining my bachelor's degree. I also feared losing the strict control I had over my eating. I begged and pleaded with my parents to give me the opportunity to overcome my disorder on my own. Finally, and reluctantly, they gave me one last opportunity to gain weight. If I failed to show improvement within a few weeks, they would proceed with their plan to seek professional help.

The threat of possibly getting off track with my educational goals and losing control over my eating snapped me out of my strange mindset just enough to change my eating habits, at least temporarily, and gain enough weight to convince my parents and even myself that I had control of my eating disorder. In hindsight, I realize that I should have accepted the offer of professional help, even if it delayed my education by a semester or two. Although at 92 pounds, I appeared healthier on the outside, I had not truly overcome my disorder on my own. As I plowed forward with my plan to get into law school, I soon resumed some of my strange and extremely unhealthy eating habits.

During my last semester at FSU, I received an acceptance letter from Stetson University College of Law in Saint Petersburg, Florida. My mom was with me when I opened the letter, and we were both ecstatic. Stetson has a great reputation and one of the top trial advocacy programs in the United States. To deliver the exciting news to my dad, I drove out to the airstrip on the farm where he worked and waited for him to land the plane. When he got out of the plane and walked over to greet me, I asked, "Do I look any different now that I'm a law student?" When my dad realized what I meant, he was thrilled, not because he wanted me to become a lawyer, but because he knew how much it meant to me.

As I graduated from FSU and began preparing for law school, my plans seemed to be falling into place and things seemed brighter—at least for a while.

NEGATIVITY CREEPS IN

When I was in college, I thought if I could only get into law school, life would be much better. Well, it didn't exactly work that way. I was certainly proud to be in law school and determined to succeed; however, it was a difficult three years for me because that was when I first began to question whether what I considered to be a "void" in my personal life would ever be filled. Oh, sure, when I was in college, I wished I had a relationship, but I knew I was young with plenty of time to meet the right person, so I did not give it much thought. In law school, however, it really started to sink in that I was alone and, for some odd reason, I began to feel I was destined to stay alone. I'm sure that stemmed from my insecurities and feelings of not fitting in. I knew I could not let my feelings of hopelessness destroy me, but the void stayed with me all three years.

In fact, my doubt, fear, and insecurities seemed to get worse each year. Those feelings were so overwhelming I thought about giving up. I was in a strange and hopeless mindset, and I found it difficult to envision a future for myself. I would have dropped out of law school, but I did not want to be considered a failure, especially after being voted "Most Likely to Succeed" in high school. I knew I would be even more miserable if I let myself down and let down everyone who believed in me. I also did not want those who doubted I would become an attorney to have a chance to say, "Well, you weren't cut out to be an attorney, anyway." I needed to prove to myself and to the world that I could do it, so I hung in there.

Music has an interesting way of affecting our mood. The music I listened to in the '80s lifted my spirits; however, by the '90s, I began listening to music that was darker and seemed to feed my negativity. But, there was one song during that time that helped me to keep going. The song was called "After the Rain" by the rock band Nelson, which was fronted by Ricky Nelson's twin sons Matthew and Gunnar Nelson. The song offered a message of encouragement for someone ending an unhealthy relationship. As I struggled with my doubt, insecurities, and feelings of hopelessness, I kept repeating the lyrics of that song over and over in my head, and it brought me some comfort as I reminded myself that this difficult time in my life was just a "rainstorm" that would pass one day if I hung on.

During law school, my weight fluctuated between 92 and 95 pounds, but I continued some of the strange eating habits I had developed in college. When I was a young kid and a teenager, I would eat just about everything and make sure it had extra cheese and butter on top. Along with my eating disorder, however, I developed some very odd eating rituals. I went through a phase when literally all I would eat was microwave popcorn. I went through another phase when all I would eat was plain pancakes. At restaurants, I would order a short stack and emphasize to the server that I wanted no butter or syrup. If they forgot and put a dollop of butter on top, which happened quite frequently, I became extremely upset and insisted that they bring me a whole new stack of pancakes. I did not feel it was an option to scoop it off because I thought the 15 or 20 calories worth of butter that had already absorbed into my pancakes put me at risk of gaining weight. I simply could not have that. My weight was the one thing in my life that I felt I still had control over.

Despite my eating disorder and feelings of hopelessness, I forced myself to try to be more social during law school because I knew it was important to have that comradery with other law students. I also thought that socializing would open new opportunities in my personal life.

Well, I did not find love during law school. With each social event, some small part of me hoped to meet someone but a bigger part of me was convinced I would not and, inevitably, I left feeling even more lonely and hopeless than before.

Later in life, I learned that being so negative had actually kept people at a distance. But in those moments as a young law student, I didn't know any other way to be. I was consumed by my insecurities, fears, and doubts.

Being in that deep of a funk in my life, I was unable to see any good that had come from my socializing. I now realize that I had some memorable experiences, but I just did not appreciate them at the time because my thoughts were centered around what I felt was missing in my life, rather than what I was experiencing at the time. It is truly a shame that I spent those years during my young adulthood so full of despair when I should have been so full of hope and excitement for my future.

A SPARK OF INSPIRATION

After graduating from law school and passing the Florida Bar exam, I hoped things would begin falling into place for me. After all, I had finally achieved the career goal I had set for myself back in high school. Much to my dismay, finding my place in the legal profession would not be easy. In fact, I spent the next few years bouncing from attorney job to attorney job, but nothing seemed to be a good fit and I continued to obsess over what I felt was a void in my life. I found myself returning to that dark place where I had been in law school, but, by then, it was even darker. Not only was I questioning whether I would ever find a relationship, I was questioning whether I would ever fit in as an attorney.

To find inspiration, I would go to theme parks to ride a ride, catch a concert, or just walk around and enjoy the atmosphere. Walt Disney World had been an escape from reality for me as a child, and it seemed to be even more so as an adult.

As I grew older, I began to appreciate Epcot, which continues to be one of my favorite parks today. I love everything about the place, but especially walking around the World Showcase. I am always amazed by the architecture, the cuisine, and the shops. I also enjoy the concerts at America Gardens Theatre, which is Epcot's outdoor amphitheater. Through the years, I have seen some of the biggest names in music perform on that very stage.

In February 2001, I caught a concert at Epcot that would go way beyond inspiring me. I had no idea who was performing or if they were even having a concert that day. My mind was racing with thoughts about my career. I was serving out my two-week notice at another law job I could no longer tolerate. I had resigned without a plan and without another job lined up. That wasn't the smartest move I ever made, but we all make mistakes along the way and, in fact, I was contemplating whether I had made the right career choice and if I should even continue being an attorney.

By the time I walked around to America Gardens Theatre, which is halfway around World Showcase, I noticed they were having a concert. As I walked closer to read the sign to see who was performing, I could not believe my eyes. Who should be performing but SISAUNDRA LEWIS?! Could that be my childhood friend? I had not seen her in eighteen years. I had to find out so I checked the concert times and made sure to get a seat in front. The moment she walked out on the stage, I knew it was her. When she began to sing, I could not believe my ears. I did not think it was possible, but her voice was even better than it had been in school. In fact, in middle school, I thought her voice was better than any artist on the radio, but when I heard her perform as an adult, I knew her voice was one of the best in the world. After Sisaundra's performance, I patiently waited near the side of the stage in hopes of speaking with her. I realized she might not remember me after eighteen years. Just as I was trying to figure out how to get a message to her, she walked out from backstage. I yelled out, "Sisaundra!" and she came over to me and, no sooner than I could utter, "I doubt you would remember me, but . . . ," she grabbed me and hugged me and said, "Elaine! Of course, I remember you!"

Sisaundra and I spent a few minutes catching up. Although our conversation was brief, we exchanged contact information. I wasn't sure if I would ever hear from her again. I soon learned she had been touring the world with Celine Dion as her backing vocalist, vocal director, and choreographer and had worked with countless other megastars. Little did I know that not only would I hear from Sisaundra again, but that reunion at Epcot would be the start of a wonderful friendship as adults. No, I did not give up my career in law. Sisaundra's success inspired me to keeping trying to get my own career on track. Once again, she was a ray of light for me just as she had been in middle school.

NEGATIVITY FINDS ME AGAIN

After an exhaustive search, I finally found the right attorney job. Unfortunately, my joy in finding gainful employment was short lived. Instead of celebrating that my career was on track, I continued to focus on what I felt was "missing" from my personal life. By then, I was in my thirties, and nothing had worked out so far. I felt as if I were under some kind of curse. I alternated between feeling hopeful and hopeless. Hopelessness was a very dark place where I knew I could not allow myself to remain. The more I focused on my fear and feelings of hopelessness, the more downhearted I became, and the more I entertained thoughts of "ending it all."

Rather than focusing on all that I had in life, I focused on what I did not have, and I was miserable. Little did I know something was about to change all that.

THE DISCOVERY OF A LIFETIME

In April 2005, I went with my mother on a trip to Columbus, Ohio, to visit her sister, Kay, and family. With my busy work schedule, I rarely visited family out of state. I felt compelled, however, to accompany my mom on that particular trip. During our brief visit, everyone ventured out to the local shopping mall. I don't really like to shop but decided to go along for the ride. When we arrived at the mall, my mom, Aunt Kay, and a few others shopped for clothes at a department store. I, on the other hand, wandered off on my own to check out the different stores in the mall. I noticed a little rock and mineral shop that piqued my curiosity, so I wandered inside. They had all kinds of rocks, minerals, and fossils. On one shelf, I noticed a box of fossils with a sign that read, "Spinosaurus Teeth: $15 each." The owner asked if he could help me.

"Are these real dinosaur teeth?" I asked. "They can't be!"

The owner assured me they were real and explained that *Spinosaurus* was a very large, carnivorous dinosaur from Morocco. At that, I wanted to know more. I decided to buy one of the teeth and do a little research on my own. Perhaps I would prove him wrong (surely the teeth were fake!) or perhaps I would discover that he was right and that I owned a tooth from a real dinosaur. Either way, I could not wait to find out more.

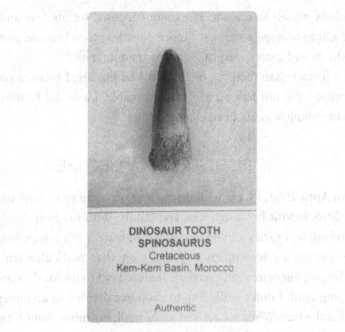

DINOSAUR TOOTH
SPINOSAURUS
Cretaceous
Kem-Kem Basin, Morocco

Authentic

Figure 5. My first *Spinosaurus* tooth

When I met up with my mom, I was excited to show her my prehistoric purchase. Her reaction was not what I expected. Instead of sharing in my enthusiasm, she questioned my judgment in purchasing something I could not prove was authentic. When I told her that it only cost me $15, she replied: "Whew! I thought you had paid several hundred dollars for it!" Knowing I had not gone into debt for it, my mom then thought my little dinosaur tooth was pretty cool. Nevertheless, my mom's initial skepticism made me even more determined to find out whether my little *Spinosaurus* tooth was real.

And like that, a transformative passion was born.

Since that fateful day, I've been on an adventure that I'm still on today.

Figure 6 *(top)*. Examining dinosaur tracks at a Wyoming Dinosaur Center dig site

Figure 7 *(left)*. People from left: Jimmy Waldron, Dean Lomax, and me visiting the DinoDigs exhibit hall at Orlando Science Center

Figure 8 *(above)*. Working in the field in Wyoming

2

BREAK THE CHAINS OF NEGATIVITY AND MAKE THAT POSITIVE CHANGE

found my life-changing passion inadvertently, and I have been enjoying the benefits ever since. If you would like to see such a positive change in your own life, don't wait for it to happen by chance. You have the power to take control. With some planning and effort on your part, you can discover your own unique passion and intentionally initiate your own positive transformation.

Once you recognize that your thoughts may be focused on negativity (like mine were), it is time to do something about it.

In this chapter, we'll examine the steps you can take to build time into your life to pursue your interests, consciously change your mental focus, and begin drawing positivity into your life.

STEP 1:
CONSCIOUSLY CHANGE YOUR MENTAL FOCUS

At any given time, just about everyone hopes for something to unfold in his or her life, be it a career opportunity, a relationship, having a child, getting into college, moving into a better housing situation, getting out of debt, saving up enough money to start a business, and so on. When pursuing a goal, we take the steps we think are necessary to make it happen, but in order for any dream to come true, there's usually a certain amount of waiting involved. During that waiting period, it is so easy to get discouraged and lose hope.

Shortly before discovering my passion—during a time when I was still focused on the "void" in my life—I was walking around an amusement park, hoping the festive atmosphere would lift my spirits. Although I had so much going on in my life, including a good job and wonderful family, I was in a state of despair. As I walked around the park with this overwhelming feeling of sadness, a thought popped into my head out of nowhere: *Don't Be in Bondage to Your Dream*.

Initially, I was not sure what it meant. Once I started thinking about it, though, it made sense. While I thought I was focused on something positive (a relationship), I had actually become more focused on worrying about when and if it would happen for me. I knew in my heart I would have a relationship one day, but I was so focused on the fact that I was not yet in a relationship that I had become a prisoner to my doubt and fear.

Negativity can be like a black hole, constantly sucking you in. Focusing on the problem is like picking at a scab on your arm. You don't provide the scab with the opportunity to heal and get better. Rather, the wound continues to fester and infection can set in. In my case, my negative focus led to increased self-doubt, fear, and hopelessness. From there, I found I was not only wallowing in self-pity regarding my personal life, but my negativity had pervaded virtually every other area of my life.

Thankfully, once I discovered my passion for paleontology, I was able to break free from my negativity. Not only did finding my passion allow me to focus my thoughts in a positive direction, it allowed me to restore my sense of hope for my future. I felt myself climbing out of that black hole that had sucked me in for far too long.

If you are a prisoner to your own negativity, it is time to break those chains and initiate a cycle of positivity in your life by changing your mental focus to something you are passionate about. When you do that, your positive energy will draw positive people and opportunities into your life, and negativity will lose its hold on you.

STEP 2:
START MOVING FORWARD

We all have busy lives—work, family, chores, and school can pull you in a million different directions. At the end of a long, 9–5 day or during those precious weekend hours, it can be hard to commit some time to yourself and to the act of fostering your interests. But, for the sake of unearthing your own happiness and passion, it's something that must be done.

I certainly did not have a lot of free time on my hands when I bought that intriguing little *Spinosaurus* tooth in Columbus, Ohio. That tooth, however, sparked an enthusiasm I had not felt in years, and I knew I had to learn more.

When I returned home to Florida, I spent every free moment I could find researching dinosaurs and fossils on the internet, and my research convinced me that the little tooth I had purchased in Columbus was indeed real. I thought such a discovery would satisfy my interest in dinosaurs, but that spark of interest refused to die out, and my fascination did not stop there. In fact, the more I researched, the more intrigued I became. So, I consciously set out to unearth more about my newfound passion and actively took some leisure time to physically explore more.

I soon discovered The Dinosaur Store in Cocoa Beach, Florida. In my quest to learn more, I made numerous trips there to talk with the owners, Steve and Donna Cayer, and their staff, whose knowledge of fossils and prehistoric life was quite impressive.

Over the next year, I also joined the Florida Fossil Hunters, where I met fossil enthusiasts Russell Brown and Bonnie Cronin, who have a passion for sharing their in-depth knowledge with others. Russell and Bonnie display their incredible collection of Florida fossils at fossil events, schools, or other public events and share their knowledge with people of all ages. Russell and Bonnie may never know the true impact they have had as they continually strive to educate and inspire.

One thing is for certain; they truly inspired me and motivated me to assemble my own small display so I could share what I was learning about dinosaurs.

Steve and Donna Cayer

In 2005, when I first became interested in paleontology but was not sure where to begin, I made my first trip to The Dinosaur Store in Cocoa Beach, Florida. At the time, it was a small fossil shop located in a shopping plaza. That was my first encounter with Steve and Donna Cayer. Back then, I was basically clueless about fossils, and Steve, Donna, and their knowledgeable staff took the time to explain the various fossils in their shop and what dinosaurs or other prehistoric creatures they came from.

Over the course of the next few years, I returned to The Dinosaur Store on a regular basis. Right before my very eyes, the store outgrew its location, and Steve and Donna built a three-story building across the street from the original site. The first floor of the new building consists of a much larger fossil and gift shop, as well as the interactive Adventure Zone for kids. On the second and third floors lives a 20,000-square-foot nonprofit museum called the Museum of Dinosaurs and Ancient Cultures. The museum houses an unbelievable collection of dinosaur fossils, skulls, skeletons, and dioramas, many from Steve and Donna's retired traveling exhibition. Both The Dinosaur Store and the Museum of Dinosaurs and Ancient Cultures are amazing reflections of Steve and Donna's passion for paleontology.

Figures 9 and 10. Museum of Dinosaurs and Ancient Cultures
in Cocoa Beach, Florida

STEP 3:

TURN AN INTEREST INTO A PASSION

In Chapter 3, we discuss what qualifies as a passion and how to identify one for yourself. Generally speaking, most passions start out as simple interests, like mine did. As I continued to pursue it, my interest grew into a passion that became a necessary part of my life.

After discovering my interest in paleontology, I spent the first couple years researching on the internet, attending fossil club meetings, and assembling my educational display. By 2007, however, I decided to take my quest for prehistoric knowledge to a new level and get some hands-on experience. Through my online research, I discovered the Wyoming Dinosaur Center (WDC), a museum in Thermopolis, Wyoming, that offered volunteer certification in fossil preparation and fieldwork. Instead of taking a vacation that year, I went to Wyoming for two weeks to learn the proper way to prepare fossils.

At the Wyoming Dinosaur Center, the staff welcomed me as I looked around in awe, particularly of their gallery. As much as I wanted to stand around and look at the exhibits, I was there to learn fossil preparation techniques, so I made my way to the prep lab where I met up with the head paleontologist/prep lab manager, William "Bill" Wahl.

In the lab, I discovered an interesting mix of people. Many were college interns from all over the world who were pursuing paleontology as a career. Others were retirees. Some of them were on an "educational adventure" through a nonprofit company called Road Scholar, and others were there to volunteer because they, too, were intrigued by paleontology.

Figure 11. Uncovering a dinosaur bone in the WDC lab

A couple who had been married more than fifty years told me they had decided to attend the Road Scholar program because they were always looking for new adventures and to expand their knowledge. Other retirees told me they come to the WDC every year or so just to learn more about paleontology.

I spent two weeks in the Wyoming Dinosaur Center's prep lab where Bill Wahl patiently showed me the proper techniques for removing rock from dinosaur bone. He also answered about a thousand questions I had for him about dinosaurs and paleontology. At the end of the two weeks, I passed the museum's test for certification in laboratory techniques. I could not have been more thrilled. Besides learning to prepare fossils, however, I learned via the retirees in the lab that age is just a number, and that we are never too old to learn and pursue new adventures.

During the summer of 2007, unable and unwilling to cap my growing interest in dinosaurs, I booked two trips to

Montana—one to the Two Medicine Formation, where the first baby dinosaurs were found in North America, and the other to the Hell Creek Formation, where the *Tyrannosaurus rex* and *Triceratops* used to roam.

For my dinosaur dig in the Hell Creek Formation, I drove out to a remote site to meet up with the paleontologist and the rest of the group. The paleontologist loaded everyone up in this truck and away we went even farther into the badlands. Upon learning about my lab training, the paleontologist chose me to help him jacket and remove *Triceratops* brow horns from the field. I had only spent two weeks with the Wyoming Dinosaur Center, and I was already being recognized for my experience.

Figure 12. *Triceratops* brow horns

By early 2008, I was anxious to return to the Wyoming Dinosaur Center, so I booked a trip for mid-May. The day I arrived in Wyoming, however, I received a call that my parents had been in a head-on collision in Florida. My first thought was to book a flight back home right then and there. But although my parents had suffered broken bones and bruises and their car was totaled, they were OK and wanted me to continue with my plans. They were excited about my newfound love for paleontology, and they knew it was changing my life before their very eyes.

Bill Wahl

William "Bill" Wahl, head paleontologist and prep lab manager at the Wyoming Dinosaur Center, which is a nonprofit museum, has been instrumental in my quest to learn about paleontology. Bill was one of the first people I met in Wyoming, and he immediately set me up in the prep lab with a dinosaur bone and began showing me how to use various tools to remove the rock from the bone. With each tool and technique, Bill emphasized the importance of not damaging the bone. Learning the proper way to prepare fossils in the lab gave me a strong foundation for fieldwork. Working around Bill in the prep lab, and subsequently in the field, was like getting a college education in dinosaur bones. I doubt anyone else could have taught me so much in so short a time. I think one of the main reasons Bill is such a great teacher and mentor is because he emphasizes that we learn by doing.

In addition to his in-depth knowledge of dinosaurs, Bill is also an expert in marine reptiles—which includes ichthyosaurs, plesiosaurs, and mosasaurs. I did not know much about marine reptiles before I met Bill, but after spending time around him, I gained a true appreciation for those amazing and mysterious animals. Bill's passion for paleontology comes through in everything he does, and especially in the way he shares his extensive knowledge with those around him.

Figure 13. In the field with
WDC paleontologist Bill Wahl

STEP 4:
GET SUPPORT AND ACCEPT MENTORS

We'll discuss sharing your passion more in Chapter 5, but when you're first trying to foster an interest, it's helpful if you build a community of people around you who can encourage and mentor you as you continue your pursuits.

Back home in Orlando, I continued to attend Florida Fossil Hunter meetings, which were held at the Orlando Science Center (OSC). It was there that I met a young man named Jimmy Waldron, who was, at the time, OSC's staff paleontologist and lead for the DinoDigs exhibit hall. From the moment I met him, it was clear that Jimmy had a passion for dinosaurs and fossils and was committed to educating and inspiring others to learn and research for themselves.

After Jimmy learned about my trips out West and my training with the Wyoming Dinosaur Center, he encouraged me to volunteer with OSC. I eagerly agreed and began volunteering a couple hours here and there, as much as my schedule would permit. Jimmy also began making trips to the Wyoming Dinosaur Center to volunteer in the lab and field and has since started a podcast called *Dinosaurs Will Always Be Awesome*, through which he not only shares paleontological discoveries but also tells the stories behind the discoveries.

Additionally, through several paleontology-related events in Central Florida, I met Chris DeLorey, who is the director of education for the Brevard Zoo in Melbourne, Florida. Chris also runs the nonprofit Academy of Natural History Preparation through which he educates teachers in the various aspects of paleontology, including fossil preparation. Chris is, hands down, one of the busiest people I have ever met, but also one of the most enthusiastic. Like my other paleontologist friends, Chris inspired me not only to learn more about paleontology, but to acquire more hands-on training and share what I was learning with others.

Encouraged by Jimmy, Chris, and the others, I decided to return to the Wyoming Dinosaur Center in August 2008 to complete my certification in fieldwork. It was then that I met an eighteen-year-old from Doncaster, England, named Dean Lomax. From the moment we met, Dean and I made a lasting friendship based completely on our mutual love for fossils. I could not believe how our shared passion broke through

Figure 14. Chris DeLorey and me at the Brevard Zoo

Figure 15. Young Dean Lomax with *Camarasaurus* femur at a WDC dig site

any barriers that might have otherwise existed on the basis of age or nationality. It was as if I had known him for a lifetime. Although he was still a teenager, Dean had an in-depth knowledge of paleontology and was determined to make it his career. With his drive and passion, I knew he would be a successful paleontologist one day.

After spending a week working in the field with Dean and the WDC staff, I took and passed the tests for basic and intermediate fieldwork. While that may not have been a degree in paleontology, it meant I had some valuable experience in the field, and I was ecstatic.

On a subsequent trip to the Wyoming Dinosaur Center, I even had the opportunity to assist Dean in taking photos for his book *Dinosaurs of the British Isles*. When it was released, I was surprised and honored to see that Dean had included my name in his list of acknowledgments. That kind gesture confirmed to me that I was making at least some small contribution toward the field of paleontology.

Figure 16. At a WDC dig site with Dean Lomax

Later, I was also honored to find that the Orlando Science Center had included a photo of me in its DinoDigs exhibit hall.

Figure 17. Photo of me in the DinoDigs exhibit hall
at Orlando Science Center

Dean Lomax

Most individuals who aspire to become a paleontologist first obtain a degree in geology, biology, or other natural science before attempting to build a career in the field. Dean Lomax's economic circumstances did not allow him to take that path. Dean's grades were not very good in school, and he simply could not afford to attend university. Instead of allowing his situation to deter him, however, Dean decided to create his own path to success. At eighteen years old, Dean sold the *Star Wars* action figures he had collected as a boy to finance his first trip to the Wyoming Dinosaur Center, where he spent months gaining hands-on experience in all aspects of paleontology. When Dean returned home to England, he continued to build upon the knowledge and experience he had gained at WDC by conducting research, writing about his discoveries, and seizing every opportunity to acquire more valuable experience.

Dean is now a multi-award-winning paleontologist, who has discovered five new species of ichthyosaur (a prehistoric marine reptile), one of which earned him a gold medal from the British House of Commons. Dean has also earned a Master of Philosophy degree from the University of Manchester and has written two books, *Fossils of the Whitby Coast* and *Dinosaurs of the British Isles*, as well as numerous scientific articles. In addition, Dean appeared as an on-camera co-presenter with British TV presenter Ellie Harrison on the popular two-part television documentary, *Dinosaur Britain*, as well as *CNN Inspirations: Wild Discoveries* with Max Foster.

Even before Dean achieved success in his field, he consistently strived to share his knowledge of paleontology with people of all ages by giving lectures at schools and museums. Today, he continues to share his expertise as well as his enthusiasm on an even larger scale through television and radio appearances, as well as through his books and speaking engagements. Dean is truly on a mission to educate others around the world about ichthyosaurs, British dinosaurs, and the field of paleontology in general.

If my passion for paleontology was strong enough to transform my life in such a meaningful way, then it is not surprising that Dean's passion for the field opened up unbelievable opportunities for him.

Figure 18. Dean Lomax at the Stuttgart State
Museum of Natural History, Germany

STEP 5:
TRUST YOUR INNER STRENGTH

Trusting in your inner strength is a skill that is developed over time. It's something that comes only after you've learned to shut out negative thoughts and self-doubt, and that comes easier once you've allowed yourself the time to build up your interests and support team around those interests. As you continue to consciously pursue your passion, you'll build up confidence in your skills and find the internal strength to perhaps branch out to something new, take a chance on a positive result, or perhaps even mentor others with similar passions.

Over time, as I dove deeper into the paleontology world, I began to discover my own creativity. To give people a better understanding of each dinosaur, I decided it would be beneficial to add cast or replica dinosaur skulls to my display. (Real dinosaur skulls are far too expensive and belong in a museum for paleontologists to study.) I soon learned, however, that even replica skulls can be quite expensive. So, I decided to try my hand at sculpting a dinosaur skull out of papier-mâché. Although I could have used sturdier material, I opted for papier-mâché because it was environmentally friendly, light weight for transporting, and has the look of bone. My first "prototype" skull turned out relatively well and, with encouragement from my family and friends, including Dean, I made more.

Although they may not be scientifically accurate, I come away from each experience not only adding a new skull to my collection, but also knowing a lot more about that

Figures 19–24. My dinosaur sculptures

dinosaur because of all the research that went into it. Perhaps most important, sculpting dinosaur skulls is a good way for me to keep my mind focused in a positive and productive direction.

STEP 6:
KEEP MOVING FORWARD AND TAKING ACTION

Life is all about attitude and perspective. Being passionate about something teaches you to keep going, to shake off the disappointment and fear, to take that big step—or those small steps—to pursue it. People who buy a lottery ticket each week make sure they have a chance to win the jackpot. For sure, everyone who has won big or even won small has had to buy at least one ticket.

Figure 25. Play to win!

I now realize it works that way with most things. If we want something good to come our way, we must take some action. During the summer after we moved to Astatula, Florida, I decided to handwrite every celebrity I could think of to ask for an autographed photo. To my surprise, I received some form of response from many of them, or at least their management company. Many celebrities sent me a photograph—either with or without an autograph (often pre-printed). Every couple of weeks, however, I opened an envelope that contained a photograph personally autographed "to Elaine." I appreciated the ones who sent me anything at all, but I was ecstatic that a select few stars, from Don Rickles to Jamie Lee Curtis, took the time to send a fourteen-year-old kid in Florida a personally autographed photo. Those autographed photos meant so much to me that I still have them today.

I would not have those photographs had I not asked for them.

Seeking employment also helped me understand the importance of taking action. When I first started applying for attorney jobs, I received so many rejection letters, it seemed I'd have a better chance of winning the lottery. But I kept applying, knowing the odds were that I'd eventually land a job, and I did. I landed a number of jobs over the course of my career, some that worked out and others that did not. The fact is that I would not have gotten any of those jobs had I not applied for them.

Relationships, too, rarely occur out of thin air. Someone must take the initiative to say hello or ask the other person on a date. If neither party takes action, there's little chance that a relationship will develop.

Remember, if there is something you want in life, approach it the way you approach your passion. Take that chance and do something about it, whether it's applying for jobs, advocating for yourself, or just striking up a conversation with someone you'd like to meet. No, not all your efforts will be fruitful, but in order to build the life you want, you must take action on a consistent basis. If you allow your fear of rejection to keep you from going after your dreams, then they will likely remain just that—dreams. No matter how many times you may feel "rejected," you must continue to take action in order for your dreams to become reality.

3

DEFINE YOUR PASSION

When I purchased that little dinosaur tooth in Columbus, Ohio, it was not only the beginning of an exciting hobby for me, it was the beginning of my passion for paleontology—and that passion literally transformed my life from one of hopelessness and despair to one of positivity, excitement, and adventure. How do you define passion? How do you distinguish between passions and simple interests? Will just any passion be strong enough to transform your life for the better? And why did finding mine have such a significant impact on my life?

In this chapter, we'll discuss four clear and concise steps you can take to define your passions, to weed out things not worth your time, and to let your true passion (not just simple interests) shine in your life. Through the years, I have taken up a number of hobbies that have come and gone without transforming my life at all. While many different pursuits or areas of interest may be called a "passion," I realized my passion for paleontology had four essential characteristics that made it powerful enough to transform my life:

1. It was positive and productive.
2. I was genuinely excited about it.
3. It was ongoing.
4. I shared it with others.

If any of those factors had been missing, paleontology would not have changed my life the way it did. Let's look at each one:

IS IT POSITIVE AND PRODUCTIVE?

The clearest and most obvious explanation for the start of my transformation is my change in mental focus, as discussed in Chapter 2. Consider this: Before discovering my passion for paleontology, I primarily focused on what I felt was missing in my life. As a result, those fears and doubts made it difficult for me to feel and be positive. Despite all the self-help books I read, I sunk further into despair. Although I had so much going on in my life, I was always "down in the dumps" and found it difficult to keep going. In short, those fears and doubts consumed me and led to negative behaviors that I (sometimes unconsciously) projected out into the world.

What I did not realize was that my negative thinking and behavior sent out negative energy, which actually repelled people from me and made it difficult for new opportunities to open for me. I was a negative black hole in the universe, if you will. People kept their distance from me to avoid being pulled in. Indeed, my negative focus had created a cycle of negativity in my life that ensured that I would never be happy or meet the right person.

For simplicity's sake, we can break this process down like this:

Focused on problem	Negative thoughts	Negative behavior	Negative consequences
Perceived void in my life	Fear, doubt, hopelessness	Wallowing in self-pity	My negative energy drove people away

However, when I turned my attention away from the emptiness and instead focused on learning more about the exciting field of paleontology, things shifted. I found myself wanting to learn more, not only for my own benefit, but for the benefit of others—the children who enjoy seeing my fossils and casts and the adults who expressed interest in learning more. In the process of learning, gathering information, and sharing my knowledge with others, I made new and amazing friends, and new opportunities opened up for me. By simply changing my mental focus to something positive and productive, I had broken the cycle of negativity and initiated a cycle of positivity in my life.

Focusing on passion	Positive thinking	Positive behavior	Positive consequences
Paleontology	Thinking of ways to learn and share	Sharing my excitement	Making new friends; opportunities opening

People who have a vice (whether drugs or gambling or whatever) would probably say they have a passion for whatever they enjoy and are addicted to; after all, they feel they cannot live without it. They may even feel it makes them "happy" when they are indulging in it. No matter how happy such a "passion" may make someone feel for the moment, if it is negative, then it will inevitably lead to negative consequences, and it will never transform that person's life for the better.

It's quite simple. Only something positive has the power to transform your life in a positive way. Once I found paleontology, it did not take long for me to realize I was pursuing something very positive. Not only that, it was productive. The more I sought to learn, the more I increased my knowledge, discovered my own creativity, educated and inspired others, and even made small contributions to the field through my volunteer work.

IS IT GENUINELY EXCITING?

While finding something positive is the first step to finding a transformative passion, you must be genuinely excited about that "something" for the transformation to take place. False excitement, even if subconscious, doesn't last; only truly genuine excitement about your passion survives the test of time.

When I was about thirteen years old, my mother, in her well-meaning effort to expand my horizons, signed me up for tap dancing lessons. When she told me what she had done, I reluctantly agreed to go to the first lesson. I knew that tap dancing was something positive to pursue, and I thought perhaps that would be the first step to learning how to dance like Michael Jackson. (Well, I could dream, right?) Once in the class, however, I felt out of place, and none of the moves came naturally to me. After the lesson, the dance teacher told my mother that I didn't seem to be "into" it and suggested that she find something that might be more suitable for me.

My mom then asked me what I was interested in pursuing. After thinking about it for a while, I told her I wanted to learn karate. I was a big fan of martial arts movies and thought it would be cool to be able to defend myself if the need ever arose. (OK, full disclosure—I really wanted to learn how to kick someone's rear end, but I soon learned that was not what martial arts were about.) My mom liked the self-defense aspect, so she agreed and signed me up at our local karate school.

Unlike tap dancing, I really enjoyed my first karate lesson, and although the moves may not have come naturally to me, I was excited to learn them and knew this was something I wanted to pursue. I quickly learned that karate was as much about mental discipline as it was about fighting techniques. I studied karate—and, later, taekwondo—for several years, eventually earning my black belt. While I stopped practicing martial arts in my early twenties, it was a passion of mine that for a few years helped me stay focused in school and truly enriched my life.

For sure, tap dancing and martial arts are both positive activities. However, I now understand that martial arts had a positive impact on my life for years, because I was genuinely excited about it. It was not until my mid-thirties that I once again found something I was genuinely enthused about that subsequently had an unbelievably positive impact on my life. If paleontology had not been of genuine interest to me, my enthusiasm would have fizzled, and it would not have had the power to change my life for the better.

Linda Blair

When I was young, the movie that scared me out of my wits the most was *The Exorcist*. Just the thought of it sent chills down my spine. In my nightmares, I saw the face of that little demon-possessed girl, portrayed by actress Linda Blair. Her portrayal was so convincing that, when I heard the name *Linda Blair*, I immediately thought of that frightening image. Well, in 1996, Linda herself would drastically change the mental image I had of her. Around Halloween of that year, my family and I went to the Disney Studios in Orlando. Much to my surprise, Linda Blair was there to greet fans and sign autographs. I decided to face my childhood fears, so I stood in line and waited my turn. Everyone in line ahead of me asked her to sign a photograph from *The Exorcist*. When it was my turn, I noticed Linda also had a photograph with her dog and cat. I told Linda that I liked the photo of her with her pets and asked her if she would sign that one for me. Linda and I then began discussing our mutual love of animals. Linda beamed with enthusiasm as she explained to me that helping animals was her passion. She told me about an organization she was working with to combat animal abuse and neglect, and she provided me with contact information. She also asked me about myself and, when I told her I was a new attorney, she wished me the best with my career and encouraged me to get involved in helping animals. My brief exchange with Linda Blair was definitely not what I had expected. Instead of coming away thinking about the horror movie, I came away inspired by Linda's genuine passion for helping abused and neglected animals, a cause near and dear to my own heart. Over the years since I met Linda, she has continued to work tirelessly as an animal advocate and founded a nonprofit organization, Linda Blair Worldheart Foundation, that rescues dogs, finds them loving homes, and works to combat animal cruelty and neglect by educating the public about important animal welfare issues. Linda not only inspires me the way she is making a positive difference in the world, she also inspired me to rescue two abused dogs, who have brought even more joy to my life.

IS IT ONGOING?

If you have found something positive and productive that you are genuinely excited about, you are definitely on the right track. However, for your passion to help you maintain a positive mental focus and to ensure that you stay on a cycle of positivity, this passion must be pursued on an ongoing, or at least a regular, basis. Certainly, martial arts were something positive I was genuinely excited about that I could have pursued for the rest of my life, but when I was in my early twenties, I allowed other things to get in the way of that passion. As a result, I stopped taking lessons and stopped practicing altogether. The same was true with my music lessons.

That stoppage allowed my mind to focus on a perceived void in my life, and the negative thoughts and behaviors crept back into my life. However, once I stumbled upon my passion for paleontology and set out to learn more about it, my mental focus then shifted back to something positive, and my life turned into an adventure that I am still on today. At the

Wyoming Dinosaur Center, I have met a number of volunteers who only discovered their passion for paleontology after they retired. They have shown me firsthand that paleontology is something I can pursue regardless of age. I also now realize that, if I were to stop pursuing something I am passionate about, I risk reverting back to negative thinking.

All this is not to say that I don't still encounter obstacles and challenges in my day-to-day life; I do. That's just part of being human. But staying positive mentally is a conscious decision that we must work toward daily; otherwise, thoughts can shift toward the negative, and off we'd go down the slippery slope again.

Max Wettstein

I mentioned in Chapter 1 that my high school science teacher, Max Wettstein, helped plant the seed for my interest in paleontology. His passion for fitness also made a lasting impression on me. In the last few years, I made a conscious decision to get in shape, and I could not help but think of Mr. Wettstein and his enthusiasm for physical fitness. Although his life ended much too soon, his passion lives on through his children. His son, also named Max, is not only an airline pilot, he is a fitness professional, consultant, and writer who has been featured in—and on the cover of—the top fitness magazines in the United States. Mr. Wettstein's daughter, Veronika, also carries on her father's legacy through her own path of yoga and holistic healing. Like their father, Max and Veronika are dedicated to educating and inspiring others to improve their health and fitness levels.

CAN YOU SHARE IT WITH OTHERS?

Perhaps the single most important way that paleontology has changed my life is through sharing it with others. Before I discovered my passion, I had a difficult time meeting new people, let alone making new friends. To make matters worse, I am naturally introverted, so even when I met someone who did not want to run from my negative energy, I had a difficult time making small talk. I found it awkward and challenging to hold a conversation with people I did not know.

As I pursued my passion for paleontology, however, I began talking with new and different people about something I was genuinely interested in and excited to share with them and, in the process, I made lifelong friendships. Through my public display tables at various dinosaur events, I met countless other individuals from all over the world. Although I may never see them again, it has been rewarding to think I may have taught them something they did not know or perhaps given them something to think about and research for themselves.

If I had limited my pursuits to researching online, reading books, and collecting fossils, I know that paleontology would not have changed my life the way it did. It was through the process of getting out there and sharing my enthusiasm that I met new friends and exciting opportunities opened up for me.

There was a time that I thought being different was a bad thing, but I now realize it has been a blessing. I still don't really fit in with any particular crowd or fit any particular mold. If I had blended in with the crowd, my life would have taken a different—and likely more ordinary—path, and I doubt I would be on this extraordinary adventure I've been on for the past fourteen years. In the process of pursuing my passion, I have learned that we do not have to be "like" other people to connect with them. We can connect with people simply by sharing something in common.

Sisaundra Lewis

Figure 26. Sisaundra and me

Even as a young girl working in the Florida orange groves with her family, Sisaundra had a passion for singing that could not be contained. Not only did she entertain my classmates and me in middle school, she lifted our spirits with her voice and her positive energy. By young adulthood, Sisaundra's vocal talents had impressed popular R&B artist Peabo Bryson, who invited her to tour the world with him as his backing vocalist and duet partner. While performing the duet *Beauty and the Beast* on tour with Peabo, Sisaundra caught the attention of Celine Dion, who asked Sisaundra to join her as her backing vocalist, choreographer, and vocal director. She traveled the globe with Celine for five world tours. Returning to Florida afterward, Sisaundra went on to become a principal vocalist for Cirque du Soleil's *La Nouba* for ten years, and, in 2014, she auditioned for NBC's *The Voice*, during which Celine even made a cameo appearance. All four celebrity coaches turned their chairs for Sisaundra during her blind audition, and she went on to finish as a top eight finalist. As founder of the Find Your Voice All-Girls Initiative, Sisaundra continues to spread positivity by sharing her unbelievable gifts with others, including mentoring 300-plus girls throughout twelve public schools in Orange County, Florida. Not only does Sisaundra motivate and empower our youth, she continues to lift spirits and increase the energy level wherever she appears.

4

FIND AND NURTURE
YOUR PASSION

GO PROSPECTING!

Did you know that, in areas that are very rich in dinosaur fossils, there may be a dinosaur skeleton buried
beneath your feet? But you will never find it unless you
take the time to do a little digging. The dinosaur skeleton is
like your hidden passion. You won't find it unless you seek

Figure 27. Dean Lomax examining bone chunks in the field

it out and uncover it. So, you may ask, how do you find a skeleton if it's buried beneath the ground? First, you go prospecting. Paleontologists go to areas where dinosaur fossils are likely to be (based on the age of the formation) and look closely on the ground for small chunks of bone. If they find only a single piece of bone, then that may not be very promising. The forces of nature, including wind and rain, may have caused that one piece of bone to end up in that location. However, when more than one bone chunk is found in a particular area, there's a good chance there is more bone buried beneath the ground.

Figure 28. *Camarasaurus* bones at a WDC dig site

What does all this have to do with finding your passion? Well, the important thing is to just start looking for it, using the criteria we outlined in Chapter 3. Think of your true passion as a dinosaur skeleton hidden beneath the surface just waiting for you to uncover it. Wherever you go, whatever you do, be on the lookout for hobbies, fields, topics, and so on that pique your interest. Just as paleontologists prospect for chunks of dinosaur bone, you can prospect for a hobby or subject that sparks your imagination and interest. Sometimes, you can't tell if a hobby or field genuinely interests you just by looking at it on the surface. Sometimes, you must examine it a little more closely to determine whether it is truly something you are interested in. Look at a variety of hobbies and fields and, when one does not interest you, move on to the next one, just as the paleontologist moves on to the next "chunk."

When prospecting for your passion, the key is to look for something that has the necessary criteria to transform your life for the better. Remember, you are looking for something that:

1. Is positive and productive.
2. You are genuinely excited about.
3. You can and will pursue on an ongoing basis.
4. You can share with others.

When you find something that has all four qualities, then you know you have found something really special that will be worth your time and effort.

When I think about it, my mother actually helped me prospect for a passion when I was thirteen years old and she signed me up for tap dancing lessons. When I went to my first lesson, I realized I was not genuinely excited about tap dancing. That experience helped me to look around—in other words, to prospect—and discover martial arts, which I loved and which helped keep my mind focused in a positive direction for many years. Unfortunately, I did not understand the importance of pursuing something I loved on an ongoing basis. Eventually, I stopped pursuing martial arts, and my mental focus shifted to something negative, which caused me to be miserable for more than a decade. I did not find another true passion until I discovered paleontology.

Do not wait to stumble upon your passion; go prospecting for it. Remember, your true, transformative passion is out there. You just have to find it.

SLOWLY UNCOVER YOUR PASSION

Once you find a passion that meets the four criteria, what should you do about it? When paleontologists find a dinosaur bone that has been buried in the earth for millions of years, they don't immediately begin removing it from the ground. To the contrary, they take the gentlest tools they have and use them to slowly uncover the fossil. First, they use a small brush to brush away the dirt from the surface of the bone. Then, they use a small pick to gently remove the rock from the bone to uncover it without damaging the bone. The more paleontologists uncover, the more they can determine what they have found.

Just as the paleontologist slowly uncovers a bone, you should slowly uncover your passion. Start by gathering research, whether online, by going to the library or bookstore, or anywhere else you can find information on the topic. Depending on what it is, you may also want to sign up for a trial lesson or attend a seminar. The more you uncover, the more you will discover whether it is your true passion.

So, why is it important to slowly uncover your passion? Once we find a hobby or topic that seems genuinely exciting, it is tempting to spend money and possibly a lot of time pursuing it up front and all at once. Since money is so hard to come by these days (and few of us have a lot of extra time on our

Figure 29. Uncovering a dinosaur bone

hands), it is best to uncover your passion slowly to make certain it is something you want to pursue wholeheartedly and on an ongoing basis before investing a lot of personal resources. There have been plenty of times when, excited about a new craze, I enthusiastically bought all the equipment, gear, videos, and so on, to make sure I succeeded in my new program, only to abandon it within a few weeks (or days) after I lost interest.

My passion for paleontology, however, was a slow reveal. I became interested when I bought my first little *Spinosaurus* tooth in 2005, but I did not go out West to dig for dinosaur bones until 2007. I didn't intentionally wait that long. It's just that my love for fossils grew naturally and, by 2007, I had a burning desire to get some hands-on experience with fossil preparation and fieldwork and to get training from real paleontologists.

And simply because something is your passion doesn't mean you have to spend every waking hour or every dime you have learning more about it. If something seems interesting to you, spend a little time learning about it before you start investing your precious resources (e.g., time, energy, money). Over time, your passion will become stronger and stronger, and it will be worth the investment of your resources. But, if you find your enthusiasm starting to subside as you learn more about it, then move on to your next discovery.

Don't Be Discouraged by Roadblocks

Figure 30. On the way to a WDC dig site

As I have pursued my passion over the last fourteen years, I continue to move forward with paleontology, even when I do not know where it will lead me. I have learned that obstacles or detours do not have to be the end of the world or cause me to revert to negative mindsets or behaviors. Indeed, when we pursue anything worthwhile, we will encounter roadblocks and obstacles along the way. We all have the option either to live life as an adventure or to live it on the sidelines. I have decided to live mine as an adventure, even if that means I will encounter more obstacles and roadblocks along the way. The important thing is to approach obstacles rationally, to stay positive, and to not lose sight of the bigger picture.

A few years after I started collecting fossils and casts, I decided I would like to have my own museum where I could display my collection for everyone to see. Swept away by my excitement, I invested my savings in a small commercial building, which I bought at a great price. I soon learned, however, that the place was not ideal for a dinosaur museum. Not only was it off the beaten path, it was just a big empty room with no plumbing. When I contacted the zoning department for my county and found out the cost of everything I needed to do to transform it into a museum, I was overwhelmed. I did not have the time or money to take on such a project. Instead of feeling discouraged, however, I put my little building on the market. To my surprise, I sold it quickly and made a nice profit. So, while I was not able to turn my building into a museum, that roadblock turned out to be a positive one.

Not all of my trips out West have turned out as I had planned, either. One year, I made plans to go on a dinosaur dig in South Dakota, just for the weekend. My mom thought the trip sounded interesting, so she decided to go as well. She had planned to do some sightseeing while I dug for dinosaur bones, then we would both visit the Black Hills Institute and Mount Rushmore. We definitely had big plans for that weekend—and no idea what roadblocks lay ahead.

After experiencing some flight delays out of Orlando, we landed in Denver, Colorado, to transfer to our connecting flight to Rapid City, South Dakota. Unfortunately, our connecting flight had been canceled due to maintenance issues, with no more flights out until the next morning. The delay would cause me to miss my dinosaur dig, which was scheduled for the following day. After discussing the options, my mom and I decided to just spend the weekend in Denver. After all, Denver has a world-class museum and zoo, which we had yet to explore. We ended up having a nice and relaxing time in Denver and, better yet, the airline refunded my money for the flight. It was not the trip we had planned, but it was a fun trip we will never forget.

Bottom line? Remember that it's OK when things do not go as planned. Whether a roadblock creates a delay or causes you to re-chart your course, the important thing is to keep moving forward and to look for ways to turn your obstacle into an opportunity.

DIG IN!

I did not comprehend how much work was involved in excavating a dinosaur bone until I started getting some hands-on experience in paleontology. One thing is for certain: the process requires paleontologists to invest quite a bit of time and energy to make sure the bone is removed from the ground properly.

Likewise, once you have found the hobby or topic you are passionate about and, after slowly uncovering it, if you are still interested and committed to learning more, then it is time to "dig in." By this, I mean it's time to invest more effort into it. For me, "digging in" included assembling my own small dinosaur display, researching as much as I could online and in books, joining a fossil club, volunteering with the Orlando Science Center, and ultimately going out West to the Wyoming Dinosaur Center to get certified in fossil preparation and fieldwork. It did not happen overnight, but that's one of the great things about your passion—you do not have to do it all at once. You can pursue it at your own pace.

DOCUMENT AS YOU DIG

Before excavating a dinosaur bone, paleontologists document as much information as possible about it, including the precise location where the bone was found and its distance and relation to other fossils found nearby. If those details are not documented before the bone is removed from the ground, that valuable information may be lost forever.

Just as paleontologists document everything they find, I suggest you document as much as possible when uncovering your own passion. Keep a written record of all the great resources and information you uncover—it'll help you in times when your memory fails you. When you read something interesting or find out the title of a good book on the topic or

Figure 31. Paleontologist Bill Wahl documenting information at a dig site

information about a volunteer organization or opportunity, write it down or save the information in a file on your computer. Also, as you make contact with others who share the same passion or who have achieved success in that area, be sure to document and save their contact information for your future reference. It will help you build a future network of like-minded friends, too. I cannot express how important my contacts have been in furthering my pursuit of paleontology. And do not be shy to call or email your new contacts whenever you have a question. You will be surprised how many people want to help you, especially when you are pursuing something they are also passionate about.

REMEMBER TO MAKE TIME
FOR YOUR PASSION

In order to find your passion and pursue it to a degree that it transforms your life, you must actually make time for it. That does not mean you must devote a lot of time to it. It just means you must make *some* time for it on a regular basis, even if it means skipping your favorite television shows from time to time. It will most certainly be worth it.

Figure 32. Beware of procrastination!

Like anything else, there may be times where you just don't "feel" like doing it or it's not convenient for you. In 2014, during a time when I was swamped with work, another attorney in my office asked if I would be willing to take an educational display to an elementary school in Georgia and share it with a class that was studying dinosaurs. As much as I love sharing my passion, that was bad timing for me because I did not feel I had the extra time to pack up my display and take it to another state. Before declining the opportunity, I reminded myself how rewarding it is to share my passion with others, especially schoolchildren, some of whom had never had the opportunity to see a dinosaur display until then. I then decided that I would make the time to share my passion with those schoolchildren. I'm certainly glad I did. The experience I had sharing my display with the class of eager dinosaur fans was priceless. And, it was an even bigger hit than I imagined. Not only did the students who were studying dinosaurs enjoy my display of fossils, casts, and sculptures, the principal allowed every student in the school to come see it. By the time it was over, approximately 500 children had stopped by, and I cannot tell you how many times that day I heard the word, "Cool!" Who knows? Maybe I inspired one of them to become a paleontologist, to take more of an interest in schoolwork, or to find his or her own passion.

KEEP LEARNING AND DIGGING

Figure 33. Chipping away at rock to uncover dinosaur bone

Yes, in order to actively pursue a passion that transforms your life, you will need to sacrifice some of your time and seize opportunities, even when it may not be convenient. However, it is through seizing those opportunities to share, teach, inspire, and meet new people that your passion will begin to truly enrich and transform your life for the better.

Jessica Lippincott

In recent years, I have had the opportunity to work in the field with not only Bill Wahl but also WDC paleontologist Jessica Lippincott, whose prior experience includes working for the Tate Geological Museum in Casper, Wyoming. During her early years, Jessica was part of the team that first began excavating Jimbo the *Supersaurus*, a 106-foot sauropod dinosaur found in Douglas, Wyoming. She also worked in the Sundance Formation, as well as the Lance Formation, where she assisted the team in excavating *Triceratops* and *Nodosaurus* fossils. In 1997, Jessica began her affiliation with the Wyoming Dinosaur Center, where she has worked in different capacities through the years, including as prep lab manager and now as dig site manager and education director. Jessica has a passion for teaching young people about paleontology, and she does so not only through her work with WDC, but also by writing about dinosaurs and other prehistoric animals. Her book, *Wyoming's Dinosaur Discoveries*, is a valuable resource that explains where dinosaur specimens initially found in Wyoming are now located all over the world. Whether she is writing, teaching, or working in the field, Jessica's enthusiasm for paleontology always shines through.

Figure 34. Paleontologist Jessica Lippincott in the field

Just as paleontologists continually study fossils to learn more about them, it is important to keep learning more about your passion. As much as I try to stay current, inevitably someone will come up to my table and ask me a question to which I do not know the answer. While it may be tempting to tell them what I "think" the answer may be, I know that would not benefit them or me, so I tell them that, while I don't know the answer off the top of my head, I will find out for them. When that happens, I end up learning something new and ensure that I'm providing the other person with accurate information. Remember, you do not have to know everything there is to know about a topic to share it with others. However, when you strive to learn as much as possible, you will be surprised how knowledgeable you become.

5

SUSTAIN YOUR PASSION
AND SHARE THE POSITIVITY

ome people ask if I am "happy" being an attorney. I've learned that being happy is a state of mind one can have regardless of his or her job. I have held a variety of jobs, from working in the legal profession to working at a theme park. I have learned that every job comes with its share of stress. Even the jobs that seem like they should be fun and carefree come with their fair share of challenges. The key to happiness is to remain positive, no matter what your job or what stressful situation you are facing. I have found that having something I am passionate about helps me to focus on something positive and, in turn, be a positive and happy person no matter what is going on in my life. Regardless of your education or what position you currently hold or wherever you are on your journey in life, *you* have the power to enjoy your life.

Now that your passion is firmly in your life, it's time to share it with others. Think of it as one big snowball effect. You enjoy doing something (your passion), which in turn makes you a more positive person. Your natural energy will turn positive, too, and, like the Sisaundra Lewises and Dean

75

Lomaxes of the world, such positive energy will rub off on others. That will exponentially increase the levels of positivity around you, and so on and so forth. People gravitate to happier, positive people.

News stories about negative people doing negative things are on a constant loop in today's media. But there are, in fact, a lot more of us in the world with something positive to share and—now more than ever—it is time for us to make sure we do just that—even if it is as simple as sharing our hobby or area of interest with others. We may not be able to do much about the negativity going on in the world, but we do have the power to create positivity by getting out there and sharing something interesting and exciting.

So, how do you sustain your passionate energy and ensure maximum positivity in your life? In this chapter, I'll offer some key takeaways to help you build up this snowball effect.

Matthew and Gunnar Nelson

Matthew and Gunnar Nelson's song "After the Rain" helped me put things in perspective during some hopeless times. I've recently had the opportunity to see them in concert—on the very same stage where I reconnected with Sisaundra. Hearing them perform "After the Rain" live—at that special place—was a moving experience for me. I was even more inspired to witness how Matthew and Gunnar have dedicated their lives to making music and, perhaps most important, keeping the memory of their father, Ricky Nelson, alive. Not only do they enjoy performing their father's music for those who grew up listening to him, they are also excited to share it with younger generations who may be hearing it for the first time. For sure, Matthew and Gunnar have given me a newfound appreciation for their dad and his music. And they continue to inspire me not only with their musical talent but with the positivity they create by pursuing their passion.

GO WITH THE FLOW
(AND DON'T FORCE THINGS)

It is amazing to watch the way the water flows down a river. Nature makes sure the water has a natural flow to it. It takes the path of least resistance. Likewise, everything that is meant

Figure 35. The Bighorn River, Thermopolis, Wyoming

to be in our lives should have a natural flow. If you find yourself trying to force something to happen in your life, it is probably not meant to be.

When I was younger and thought I had met the right person, or was applying for my dream job, I would go to any lengths to try to make the situation work. However, it seemed the more I tried to force those situations, the less likely they were to work out for me. And, when things did not work out as I had hoped, I would become terribly discouraged. I now realize that the situations that were not meant to be in my life were simply not going to work out, no matter how hard I tried. Trying to force those situations was an exercise in futility that only brought me down further.

On the other hand, the people, jobs, and situations in my life that *were* meant to be had a natural flow to them, and I did not have to force them. Of course, even when going with the flow, you will face challenges that require you to put forth your best efforts to overcome them. However, when you invest 100 percent of your efforts into a situation, it should improve and progress naturally. When it does not, it may be time to move on.

I have since learned the importance of letting go and going with the flow in all areas of my life, even my real estate transactions. When I sold my commercial property, I decided to make an offer on a small house on a lake near my parents' home. To ensure that my offer would be accepted, I offered more than the asking price. I was so sure the seller would accept it. Much to my dismay, my realtor advised me that the seller accepted another offer. At first, I was upset, but I reminded myself that, if it was not meant to be, I needed to let it go. I decided then not to worry about it and to continue looking until I found the house that was meant for me.

To my surprise, a few weeks later, the little lake house was back on the market. The other buyer had backed out. I called my realtor and told him to put in an offer for the asking price—not one dime more. I decided if I was meant to have the house, things would work out and, if not, I would let it go again. To my amazement, the seller quickly accepted my offer, and I ended up closing on it in less than a month. At that point, the transaction had a natural flow to it. It is so strange that, when I felt desperate to purchase the house and even offered more than the asking price, the deal fell through. However, when I stepped back and let it go, then everything fell into place. The house was meant to be mine, so my willingness to let it go did not stop the natural flow of things; it simply gave me the peace of mind to accept whatever was meant to be.

Don't force something that does not have a natural flow to it. Just learn to let go, "go with the flow," and keep moving forward in a positive direction. And remember that losing something that is not meant to be in your life is not an ending, but a necessary step toward a new beginning.

SEE YOURSELF AS A WINNER

Through the years, I learned that the way we label ourselves plays a big role in how we see ourselves and, in turn, what we end up achieving in the long run. For instance, when I was very young, I was confused about my own capabilities after being placed in a group for slow learners and struggling with math, English, and science. My mind was so unfocused that I consciously decided that I would just be an "average" student. For that period, I did not see myself as anything more than

Figure 36. I am dino-mite!

average, and I did not have any big aspirations for myself. I just wanted to play video games and get by in school without receiving negative attention.

That mentality of "just getting by" all changed when I received positive feedback from my high school teachers and began to realize my own potential. I was still the same person with the same capabilities, but those teachers helped me to see myself as a successful student with a promising future. Once I saw myself as a successful person, I began living up to that by consistently making the honor roll and taking an active role, including leadership positions, in extracurricular activities. At fifteen years old, I began mapping out my plan for success and, although I had a challenging road ahead of me, I ultimately achieved my goal of becoming an attorney. I often wonder what I would have become had I never changed the label I had placed on myself from "average" to "successful." For sure, I would have limited my own potential.

I have learned that there is no magic in becoming successful. It takes hard work and determination and, most important, not giving up. I have learned that is the formula for success for just about anything we do in life. No matter who you are or what stage you are at in life, make sure you see yourself as a success, get a plan, and follow through with it, even when the going gets tough. When you know you are a winner, there is no limit to what you can achieve.

SEEK OUT THOSE WHO BUILD YOU UP

After I discovered my love for paleontology, I attempted to be in a relationship with someone who constantly put me down. This person seemed nice in the beginning, but soon began criticizing my looks and personality and everything about me. That was painful to hear, especially from someone I thought cared about me. I tolerated it for a while; however, I soon realized that I did not need someone in my life who sought to tear me down. A person like that only serves to drain your energy and leave you feeling down. And when you feel down, it is much more difficult to be positive and productive, and it is especially difficult to be an inspiration to others.

There are people in this world who will see the goodness in you and want to see you go far, and then there are people out there who will strive to tear you down. While we cannot totally avoid the people who want to tear us down, we can make sure to not let them get inside our heads and steal our joy or limit our potential. We can also actively seek out those who build us up, who inspire us with their own passion and positivity. We all have the power to make a difference in the world, to inspire others, and to make our lives an exciting adventure. In order to do so, we must maintain a positive mindset. When I was full of despair and feeling bad about myself, I was miserable and, even when I got my career on track, I doubt I inspired many people because I was still unhappy and continued to question my self-worth.

Thankfully, discovering my passion for paleontology has helped me overcome my negative thinking. Besides keeping my mind focused in a positive and productive direction, paleontology has given me the opportunity to make some really great friends, like Dean Lomax, who always encourages and inspires me to move forward. Dean has also expressed to me that he appreciates our friendship as much as he appreciates my enthusiasm for fossils. I draw positivity from other close friends, like Sisaundra, whose support and encouragement has been invaluable to me. And words cannot express how supportive my parents have been throughout my life and in every area of it. Even when it seemed I had lost my way, they never gave up on me and never let me give up on myself.

I am the same person who someone found fault with on every level, and yet, there are people out there who value me and appreciate me on every level. The same is true for everyone. I can assure you there are people out there who think you are awesome—inside and out—and who recognize your worth and potential and want nothing more than to see you succeed in life. There are, however, other people out there who are quick to point out your flaws and keep you down. Do not allow the latter group to determine your future.

If you don't feel as though you have anyone in your life who sees your qualities and potential, then that is all the more reason for you to find your passion and go out and share it with others. Once you do that, you will inspire others and start drawing the right kind of people to you. Be passionate in what you do, and your world will form around you. I know that for a fact because, through paleontology, I have met such wonderful friends who have encouraged me to expand my knowledge and share it with others and, by doing so, I have drawn even more positive people to me.

Seek out those people who can help you be the best you can be. Recognize those individuals, appreciate them, and maintain your relationships with them because they are a powerful force in your life.

Focus, Focus, Focus!

Figure 37. Mapping dinosaur bones

The more we understand the power of mental focus, the more we can use it to our advantage in all areas of our lives. By 2014, I was enjoying my life so much that I soon realized I had gained 20 pounds. In fact, I found

I was unable to wear most of the clothes in my closet. In an attempt to camouflage the extra pounds, I would layer my clothing and wear a lot of black. Even if it was not obvious, I knew I had gained the extra weight, and I could not seem to shed the additional pounds. I tried eating salads, counting calories, but nothing seemed to work. The joy I experienced in eating food always won out over my desire to lose weight, and I would end up "blowing" my diet every time. It seemed I would have to carry a "spare tire" around my midsection for the rest of my life.

It then occurred to me: If I *focus* on becoming fit, then I will become fit.

I began to understand that my prior attempts to lose weight were not successful, because I was not really focused on any specific fitness goal. Oh sure, I may have set a basic goal to lose 15 or 20 pounds, but I did not have a clear, powerful image in my mind of what I wanted to achieve. Consequently, and despite the adjustments in my diet (more salad, less calories, etc.), I did not see any real results.

Mental focus was the key to my success, and I knew I needed to focus on a specific fitness goal that would genuinely excite me. So, rather than saying I wanted to lose 20 pounds or fit into a particular pair of jeans, I rummaged through fitness magazines until I found photographs of individuals who were in tip-top shape and the size I wanted to be. I then planted those images in my head and focused on getting into similar shape.

Once I began focusing on such a specific goal, I found it easier to stick to a workout routine, since I knew what

I was striving to achieve. What's even more amazing is that I did not have to eat a lot of salad or restrict my calories in order to see results. Rather than eating like a rabbit, I began to eat a high-protein diet to promote muscle development, which also helped me feel full. After a few months on a program of consistent exercise and high protein, I lost 20 pounds and found myself in the best shape of my life. No, I'm not in as good a shape as the individuals in the fitness magazines, but I'm in much better shape than before.

What are *you* focused on? Whatever it is, make sure you are using the power of mental focus to achieve the best results possible in your life.

SEIZE EVERY MOMENT

On a recent trip to the Wyoming Dinosaur Center, I was reminded how important it is to keep the adventure going and make the most of each day. On my short flight from Denver to Casper—when the plane was about 25,000 feet in the air—the pilot made an unexpected and rather alarming announcement. He said, "Ladies and gentlemen, I'm afraid I have some bad news. The aircraft is experiencing a mechanical issue that will require me to turn the aircraft around and return to Denver for repair." He did not state what the "mechanical issue" was, but that is definitely not something you want to hear a pilot say when your plane is mid-air. What if the engine stopped? What if the pilot was unable to land the plane safely? While those thoughts did cross my mind, I decided not to worry about that and just trust that we would arrive safely. And, that is exactly what happened. I must say, however, that nerve-wracking flight back to Denver reminded me how fragile life is and how things can change in an instant. I had no guarantee that the plane would land safely. In fact, no one is guaranteed to be here tomorrow. That is why it is so important to make the most of today.

I never want to take life for granted again or miss one opportunity to make the most of it. Whether I have one day left or another half-century, I plan to live it to the fullest and to stay on my ongoing quest to learn and share and to encourage others to do the same. While it is exciting to think I have inspired someone to learn more about dinosaurs and paleontology, it is perhaps even more rewarding to think I have encouraged someone to embark on his or her own unique adventure toward happiness.

KEEP THE ADVENTURE GOING

Thinking of all the excitement and opportunities paleontology has brought me, I cannot help but wonder what would have happened had I never stumbled upon my passion. I would have certainly missed out on many years of adventures and wonderful new friends. I would have also continued my pattern of negative thinking and continued to dwell on what I felt was missing in my life rather than something positive and exciting. I have learned from experience that pursuing something you are excited about can change your thoughts from negative to positive and, like a strong magnetic force, draw wonderful things into your life.

If you are stuck in a rut or focused on your negative circumstances, it is time to break that cycle of negativity. Don't wait. Go out, explore, find your passion, nurture it, and set out on your own life-changing adventure. Above all, never give up. Life itself is an adventure, and I am living proof that life does not have to be perfect to be amazing. Just keep moving forward, keep the positives flowing, and keep sharing your passion and positivity with others. With that powerful momentum, you are sure to draw the best things possible into your life!

ACKNOWLEDGMENTS

Special thanks to Tanya—without your support and encouragement, this book may never have materialized.

I would also like to express my love and gratitude to my family, who has been behind me every step of the way.

Sincere thanks also to the individuals featured in the book: Dean R. Lomax, Sisaundra Lewis, Chris Juergensen, Basil Bain, the Wettstein family, William "Bill" Wahl, Jessica Lippincott, Steve and Donna Cayer, Linda Blair, Matthew and Gunnar Nelson, Jimmy Waldron, Chris DeLorey, Russell Brown, and Bonnie Cronin. You never cease to inspire me. The way you pursue your passion has formed the very foundation for this project.

I would also like to express my sincere appreciation to the following organizations and individuals who have contributed to this book in some way, be it big or small:

The Wyoming Dinosaur Center, Angela Guyon, Levi Shinkle, Daryl Schafer, and the many other WDC staff members and volunteers who have helped and/or inspired me along the way, Teewinot Photography, David Michael Photography, the Florida Fossil Hunters, Orlando Science Center, Jeff Stanford,

Jennine Moser, Laura Harland, the Academy of Natural History Preparation, the Brevard Zoo, the Museum of Dinosaurs and Ancient Cultures, Road Scholar, Stacie Fasola, Freddie Belton, Sue Crumpton, Reid and Sandra Howard, Mary Davis, Kay and George Nickolson, Toni Cunningham, The Bain Law Firm P.L., Linda Blair Worldheart Foundation, the Two Medicine Dinosaur Center, David Trexler, and Peter Larson.

Last but not least, thanks to Radius Book Group, Mark Fretz, Evan Phail, Katie Benoit Cardoso, Lisa Kirk, Pauline Neuwirth, Jeff Farr, and the design and production team at Neuwirth and Associates for their help in bringing this project to life.

PHOTO CREDITS

Figures 1, 2. © Reid Howard.

Figure 3. Courtesy of Chris Juergensen. © Chris Juergensen.

Figure 4. Photograph by David Michael Photography. Courtesy of Basil Bain and David Michael Photography. © Basil Bain.

Figures 5, chapter 2 opener, 12, 19, 20, 21, 22, 23, 24, 25, 32, 35, 36. Photographs by Elaine Howard. © Elaine Howard.

Figures 6, 8, 11, 28, 29, 30, 33, 37. Courtesy of the Wyoming Dinosaur Center.

Figure 7. Photograph taken in the DinoDigs exhibit hall at Orlando Science Center. Courtesy of Orlando Science Center, Jimmy Waldron, and Dean Lomax. The original Stan the *Tyrannosaurus rex* skeleton is on exhibit in The Museum at the Black Hills Institute in Hill City, South Dakota.

Figures 9, 10. Photographs taken at the Museum of Dinosaurs and Ancient Cultures. Courtesy of Steve and Donna Cayer.

Figures 13, 31. Courtesy of Bill Wahl and the Wyoming Dinosaur Center.

Figure 14. Courtesy of Chris DeLorey and the Brevard Zoo.

Figures 15, 16, 27. Courtesy of Dean Lomax and the Wyoming Dinosaur Center. © Dean Lomax.

Figure 17. Photograph taken in the DinoDigs exhibit hall at Orlando Science Center. Courtesy of Orlando Science Center.

Figure 18. Photograph taken at the Stuttgart State Museum of Natural History, Germany. Courtesy of Dean Lomax. © Dean Lomax.

Figure 26. Courtesy of Sisaundra Lewis.

Figure 34. Courtesy of Jessica Lippincott and Levi Shinkle. © Teewinot Photography.

Photographs not otherwise designated are © Elaine Howard.

INDEX

ABOUT THE AUTHOR

Despite her academic struggles, low self-esteem, and battle with an eating disorder, Elaine Howard eventually achieved her goal to be an attorney. Instead of celebrating her accomplishment, however, Elaine continued to question her self-worth as she focused on negativity. Then, in 2005, Elaine inadvertently discovered her passion for paleontology, and her life was never the same. Over the past fourteen years, Elaine has become certified in fossil lab and fieldwork by the Wyoming Dinosaur Center, been on many dinosaur digs, assembled her own educational display, and made friends from all over the world. While Elaine is still an attorney, she spends her spare time as an adventurer, continually pursuing her passion for dinosaurs and other prehistoric creatures. She is also on a mission to encourage others to find their own unique passion and allow it to transform their lives into an exciting adventure.